7/00

A Little Secret
for Dealing
with
TEENS

A Little Secret for Dealing with TEENS

JENNIE HERNANDEZ HANKS

Health Communications, Inc.
Deerfield Beach, Florida

www.hci-online.com

Cataloguing-in-Publication data is on file with the Library of Congress.

ISBN 1-55874-757-5
©2000 Jennie Hernandez Hanks

Publisher: Health Communications, Inc.
            3201 S.W. 15th Street
            Deerfield Beach, FL 33442-8190

Acknowledgments:
Emily Isbell, Kurt Hanks (illustrator), and Henry Gunter
Cover design by Lawna Oldfield
Inside book design by Dawn Grove

To My Children,
Who Have Helped Me Grow Up

CONTENTS

Overheard comments from teenagers.

INTRODUCTION: I'VE BEEN THERE!

My older children became teenagers (with still more teenagers coming) during a very difficult time. My marriage was dissolving. The children were not doing well in school; for a couple of years, they weren't even attending. My husband had limited work, and we had no money. Daily, things grew worse.

Eventually my husband and I separated, and the load was totally on me to make things work. Soon I had to deal with things such as no heat in the house because I didn't have the money to buy fuel. I gathered wood scraps from a construction site and burned them in the fireplace to warm the house. Our landlady was trying to evict us even though our rent was paid. Now that there was no "man" around the house to fix things up for free, it seemed she wanted someone else to live there. My children were not dealing well with the chaos which was everywhere in their lives. Looking back, I have no idea how we made it through it all, but we did.

When I finally gained a divorce, with sole custody of seven children, we all relocated to a different state where we could get a brand-new start. I was a single mother with seven children, three of them teenagers, two of them preschoolers. Our family savings was the change we found under the sofa cushions. With no income or child support, I had to rely on government welfare to provide the basic necessities for my family. Since I had no marketable job skills, I enrolled in college as a full-time student. This was very difficult, since I had to put my younger children in daycare—something I had never done before. All this change and disruption was very confusing for my children. They weren't happy, especially my teenagers who had become angry and resentful. I could see in their eyes how they felt: "This is all your fault, Mom, that we're in this mess!"

At this point, something snapped inside me. I realized that I did not want my kids' lives to suffer because of some of my past choices. In fact, I wanted to help them have lives that were better than mine. I wanted to empower them. I needed to find a way to accomplish this.

STRETCHED TO THE LIMIT AND BEYOND

I had been a stay-at-home mom and out of the workplace for years. My physical, financial and emotional resources were stretched to the limit. I had no choice but to go back to school full time, even though I knew that the demands on my time and energy would be enormous. In addition to commuting to classes and doing schoolwork, I did all the household and parenting tasks. Whenever anything in the house broke, I was the one who fixed it. Whenever the kids had to go somewhere, I was the one who took them. The entire responsibility for raising seven children was mine alone. My teenagers especially needed more and more of my attention. All their problems, demands, concerns and self-absorptions were directed at me. They had a lot of anger because our family was apart and we were moving again. I had policemen at my door because my son was messing around with some of his friends. I couldn't keep a handle on everything by doing things the way I had in the past. My older kids were headed down a road that needed to be changed. We had problems and I needed solutions— yesterday.

I began by turning to the "experts." What I soon learned was that the "experts" usually gave complicated, long-winded instructions on how to raise teenagers. But surprisingly, many had no firsthand experience with teens. One self-proclaimed expert I saw on a talk show had all the proper credentials, yet he hadn't been married or had kids. He had *some* good ideas, but I couldn't even begin to relate to him. This seemed crazy to me, but the demands of my situation made me press on for solutions. When I read books promising answers, it often seemed that they never really got to the point. I remember one book in particular (one of the better ones, actually) that went through a twelve-step process on cooperative problem-solving with your teenagers, with page after page of technical explanations. Not very helpful. I didn't have the time or patience to read through it all and to try to apply it. I believed there had to be a better way, one that a busy, pressured parent like myself could use.

MOTHER INVENTION

I've heard that necessity is the mother of invention. I had a very real, urgent need for an effective and easy way to deal with my teenagers and help their lives (and mine) work better. I filled that need by developing an approach of my own. It's a simple, straightforward one that works with my own children, and works very well.

Today my children are thriving. My two older ones are members of the National Honor Society and Who's Who Among High School Students, and they both received scholarships to the

National Young Leaders Conference in Washington, D.C. My oldest son recently finished a term working as a page in the Idaho State Legislature and is now attending Princeton University on a full four-year scholarship. My oldest daughter graduated with high honors and was a speaker at her graduation. She also was selected to attend Girls' State, a week-long program at the State Capitol in which select girls, chosen to represent all parts of the state, learn about the legislative process. Last year she was first runner-up in the county Junior Miss Pageant and received scholarships in four categories. My younger children are now working toward similar achievements. But most importantly, our home is more peaceful and my children are learning to be responsible members of the family. What's really incredible is that they are nice people (even as teenagers!), and they are happy.

People have asked me what I did to make our family life successful. The following pages explain the process I used, which I have developed into a seminar that I give today to other parents of teens. In a way, my approach is from a "manager's" point-of-view, where getting things to work well is the driving force. This approach is based on five concepts that define our relationships with our teenagers:

- *All relationships are exchanges.*
- *Exchanges are run by rules.*

- *Some rules governing exchanges are hidden.*
- *Put all the rules on the table.*
- *Focus on getting exchanges to work.*

As you use this five-part approach, you will see your teenagers assume responsibility for their lives. They will use their creative energy in positive ways to establish relationships that work for them, particularly their relationship with you. You may not believe it yet, but you will see less contention in your home. Your children will exercise better judgment. They will mature gracefully and be ready for the world when it is time to leave home. Your life as a parent will be more pleasant.

PLEASE REMEMBER, I'M JUST A MOM

Just so you know, I'm not a psychologist, therapist or child counselor. I'm a mom. Yet many of the concepts in this book are colored by my training and interest in human resource development from a business standpoint. As I took classes on these subjects, I began applying the same principles to my family life. I found business management to be a better resource than all the child development materials I studied. In business, the bottom line is getting things done efficiently and effectively. Business is biased towards results and performance—and not necessarily concerned with the "why" of things. I didn't have the time or resources to give in to the many demands of my children, nor did I want to just leave them to their own devices. I was alone and gone most of the time. Getting my family up and running was my primary motive. To be blunt, getting through each day without a disaster was often all I wanted to accomplish. But, something miraculous happened along the way. By following this management-like path, our family slowly changed. Today, we are happier, healthier, more purposeful people. There is a delightful quality in our home, and my teenagers are all doing great.

Throughout this book, I use stories to illustrate my concepts for dealing with teenagers. Many of these stories are experiences from my personal life and the lives of others I know.* Hopefully you can relate to them and use them as reference points in your own parenting adventures. As you read and apply these concepts, please use them in a way that will uniquely benefit *you* and *your* family. The choices I used for my children may not be the same ones you want for yours.

*I have changed the names of these people throughout the book.

For example, one parent came up to me after I taught a seminar and said she liked the class but didn't agree with what I wanted from my children. I was sorry that I hadn't made it clear to her that I didn't want to impose my agenda as a parent on anyone. Likewise, the intention of this book is to give you valuable parenting tools, not showcase my ideas of what good parenting is. How you use these tools is entirely up to you and will depend on what you want for yourself and your teenagers.

Teenagers can be a real joy—fun to have around the house and even interesting. But sometimes they can be the total opposite of these things.

THE TYPICAL PROBLEM IN BEING A TEENAGER'S PARENT

Someone once told me that God gave us our children as cute little babies—so we would want to keep and take care of them. Then eventually they would become teenagers—so we would want to get rid of them. How many of you remember holding your infants and believing that these little souls would be nothing but perfect as they grew up? But somewhere along the way, you began to feel as if you were in an episode of *The X-Files* and some strange alien being had taken over your perfect child. In other words, your child began to act like a teenager.

A few months from now, I will be the parent of four teens, and I actually like them—a lot. Even so, there are times I wish that I could be taken away on the alien mothership (pun intended).

Nothing—but experience—can prepare a parent for what happens during the teen years. Being awakened suddenly by the phone ringing at 2 A.M. Hearing your four-year-old yelling for his older brother after he answers the door and a policeman is standing there. Getting into your only car to go to work and noticing the front end has been rearranged. Smelling alcohol on the breath of a teen who won't talk. Telling your kids something that will help them a great deal, only to see them turn away in complete disdain and say, "Yeah, whatever." Staring at a face you find vaguely familiar, but not quite linking the name to the face because the makeup is on too thick. Seeing your brand-new shoes on another's feet headed out the door going towards high school. And to top it all off, hearing heavy panting in the night and asking, "What's going on?!" You see two disheveled people appear—your kid and a member of the opposite sex. All this, and more, are part of raising a teen.

Realizing that many of these behaviors are "the nature of the beast," I tried to accept what was going on as a way of life. The only problem was that I already had too big a load to carry, and I didn't want to add the extra burdens of my teenagers' behaviors. I began to realistically look at what it was that I was *really* doing with my children. In business, any company that wants to succeed needs to take stock of where it is, where its resources are going and where its current direction will take the company. I decided to do the same with my family, starting with my eldest teen.

ONE TEENAGER'S EXPECTATIONS

Paul, my then-seventeen-year-old son, began to complain about needing nicer clothes and more access to the family car. He became really upset with me and what he saw as my neglect. He sent me subtle messages. A word here and a comment there. And then there is that *look*. I began to fall into the trap of feeling guilty, especially since I was either gone from the house or busy most of the time. At first I felt that I should comply with my son's demands.

After all the not-so-subtle hints, Paul and I sat down together to discuss the matter of my neglect. I suggested that we make a list of the expectations we had of each other. I wrote the list, which went something like this. He wanted me to furnish him with a room of his own with restricted access by other family members. He wanted free access to the family car—fully fueled, repaired and always clean. He wanted me to pay the auto insurance, which was dramatically more expensive because he was driving my car in the first place. He also wanted free access to my computer, including the Internet connection. He expected me to buy his clothes, but of course only the clothes he approved of. (His shoes needed to be a certain brand and style, including special shoes for each of the sports he played.) I was expected to do all of his laundry including, those times he needed that special T-shirt washed, and I had to food shop, cook and serve him all of his meals.

Pointing to the list, I asked him, "What do I get in exchange for all this?" I saw shock covering his face. He was speechless. I continued. "So I guess what you're saying to me is that I'm supposed to give all this to you in exchange for which you bless me with your presence in our home."

"Well, y . . y . . yeah!" He stammered, wide-eyed and innocent.

"Would you like to be on the other end of an exchange like this one?" I asked.

First he looked at me, then he stared into space. He could see I wasn't going to go on until he responded. Finally he admitted, "Well, no, I wouldn't."

THE $3 MILLION KID

Part of the reason being the parent of teens can be frustrating at times is that you can never consistently predict what they may do next. Often it can really be fun or interesting, but sometimes they can throw a real curve at you.

When I read in the paper that there was going to be an open auction on the Internet I immediately knew that some teenager would fool around with it. I'm not joking, and there is really no way to check the credibility of online bidders. Here a company was going to auction off many expensive items: Did they really think that no teenager was going to be tempted to try his hand at buying some of this really cool stuff? Guess what happened?

Andrew, age thirteen, who lives in New Jersey, didn't have the money to actually buy a 1955 red Ford convertible or a Van Gogh painting, or the first Superman comic book, or any of the other stuff listed with the Internet auction house. But that didn't stop Andy; he bid anyway. His mom got the bill. It was $3 million. Andy's allowance didn't quite cover a bill that large. But to him it was a game, and you know how teenagers like to play games. For his shocked parents, however, it was no game.

One item he bought was an 1860s bed which was put up for auction at $1,000 by the auction house. Then an additional thirty-three bids raised the price to $12,000, until Andrew joined in. "Andrew came in with his bid and pretty much blew everything out of the water," the director of the auction house told the media. Andrew's bid: $900,000! If he had gotten the bed, and if he is like my sons, Andy wouldn't have made the bed anyway.

Needless to say, Andrew was denied his Internet privileges. Being a minor and with all the media coverage, his parents didn't have to pay the $3 million, but look at all the hassle and embarrassment they had to go through.

When I told a friend of mine about this story, he replied, "I know what you mean. One day, as I was working out in the yard, my seventeen-year-old son asked to go to his friend's house around the corner for the afternoon. I said that was fine. Before I knew it, a couple of hours had gone by and the phone was ringing. My son was calling to tell me he had just wrecked the car and that he was 150 miles away from home. This whole time I thought he was just around the corner!"

Teenagers surprise you with this kind of stuff all the time. There you are, a diligent parent, working and making a living for your kids, taking care of things and BAM! Suddenly out of nowhere your teenager hands you a surprise.

THE LOPSIDED RELATIONSHIP

Almost all teenagers expect this same kind of a lopsided exchange with their parents. My son Paul, an honor student who seldom gets into trouble, was no exception. Teenagers naturally tend to be self-absorbed. Sometimes they don't even see that there is another side to things—the parent's side. This reminds me of a joke I once heard: "How many teenagers does it take to screw in a light bulb? One, because the teen would hold the bulb in the socket and expect the world to revolve around him."

The reality is that some teens are easier to deal with than others. Some contribute more than others. Yet all parents of teens can probably use some assistance to help their children see what their parents really do for them. What follows is a simple five-step process to help you teach your teenagers to see both sides of the relationship they have with their parents.

"My teenaged kid walks around all day in his own little world, oblivious to anything and everything. It's like he's wearing a bucket over his head."

A mom talking about her teenaged son.

The Little Secret for Success with Teenagers

For the first twenty years of your child's life, you have about seventy-three hundred days to spend with him or her—plenty of time in which to experiment and try something new when things aren't working. I've heard that the definition of insanity is to keep doing the same thing over and over while expecting different results. Yet that's what I see many parents doing with their teenagers—the same thing over and over, expecting the relationship to improve.

Many parents never really question what they're doing or why they keep doing it. It's as if they say to themselves, "What I'm doing isn't working very well, so maybe doing more of it will work better." As for me, I admit I've also made the same mistake with my teenagers, but I've learned a few hard lessons along the way. I can spend only a certain amount of effort pounding my head against an immovable object; then I figure out it's time to try another way. Now I go by this simple but often overlooked rule: *If what you're doing isn't working, try something different.*

I know what it is like to fail with my kids even after my best efforts. I know what it is like to want a better relationship with my children, a better family life, and not know what to do to get it. And I really know how hard it is to try something new. But let's face it: If what you're doing in your relationship with your teenager isn't working as well as you'd like, maybe it's time for a change. My approach to dealing with my teenagers was to try something completely different. I believe it can work for you, too.

Parents and teenagers typically *focus* on each other when interacting.

The little secret is to *focus* on improving the exchanges between each other.

A SIMPLE SHIFT IN FOCUS

This is the secret that has worked for my family: By shifting the focus to the exchange rather than on the individual, things really do begin to change. There are five steps that you can use to help you make this change. I have found it interesting that such a simple concept can make such a major shift in relationships.

SUDDENLY! SHE TURNED INTO A TEENAGER

Let me give you a quick example of what I'm talking about. This story may seem simple to you, yet the results I experienced are more valuable than I could ever say.

I have a daughter who is ten. She acts very much like she is sixteen. I'm not sure if kids are growing up faster now than before or if it is just her. Perhaps part of what happened is she is in the middle of seven children and sometimes gets lost in the shuffle. About a year ago, she began acting "older." Her interests began to change. She wanted different clothes. She constantly wanted to use the phone. The list goes on and on.

As she began to change, I think she wanted me to change with her. She wanted to be the center of attention; she wanted me to treat her that way. Well, with all that I had going on, I really couldn't always make her the center of attention. She began to get angry with me, even to the point of calling her father and "telling" on me. He would call me back to find out why I was being so mean, but there really wasn't anything in particular that she said I was doing. She would keep to herself and wouldn't participate with the family. For a while I just kind of ignored her, hoping the behavior would go away. But it didn't; in fact, it just got worse.

Now there is a change. She likes being with the family a lot.

She helps with the work at home. She likes to do things with her sisters. She and I have fun together. No more phone calls to her dad. She seems genuinely happy. How did this happen? In the pages that follow, I will share some concepts that I have applied with my children. The preceding story is really true. As I applied these principles, change occurred and things are different.

It's not a difficult change, but it will require some awareness and effort on your part. Mostly, it's a matter of changing the way you think about relationships and seeing the interaction between you and your teenager in a different light. The secrets are five simple steps, each of which builds on the one before it.

ALL RELATIONSHIPS ARE EXCHANGES.

The relationship you have with your teenager is an exchange.

Parent   **Teenager**

You give things to your teenager and expect things in return.

Your teenager expects things from you and may give the oddest stuff or nothing in return.

It is a reciprocal arrangement, each person exchanging with the other.

STEP ONE:

ALL RELATIONSHIPS ARE EXCHANGES

Suppose you go shopping at your favorite grocery store, and you discover that there aren't prices posted anywhere. After you fill your cart with groceries and take it to the checkout counter, the clerk scans your items and charges your ATM card without telling you what you spent. How long would you continue shopping at that kind of store? The reason we shop at a particular store and return to shop there again is because we have agreed on an exchange: a certain price for the products we purchase. We benefit from the exchange, and so does the merchant. We are able to shop with confidence because we know in advance what the exchange is.

Similarly, in their relationships with their teenagers, most parents are like shoppers at the imaginary "no prices" grocery store. They engage in exchanges with their teenage children without ever looking at the cost involved.

I'm not asking you to turn your relationships into exchanges; I'm asking you to recognize that all of your relationships are already exchanges. We engage in exchanges with grocers, bankers, hairdressers, teachers, spouses, kids and pets. We exchange things such as money, goods, services, time, energy and companionship. We also exchange less quantifiable things, such as friendship, love and fulfillment. Regardless of the content of the exchange, all of our relationships involve some kind of exchange. Let's look at some common exchanges.

A FRIENDLY EXCHANGE

Cathy has been my friend for years. Our exchange is easy to see. We both have shared similar experiences in our lives. We understand each other and can talk for hours together. I have used her as a sounding board to help me work out problems or concerns I have, and she does the same with me. Cathy has been the only friend I have had at times and has helped me through some rough experiences. I have done the same for her. We may not have contact for months at a time, but with a phone call, we immediately start again where we left off. Our friendship works because we both benefit from the exchange. I've helped her. She's helped me. I listen to her. She listens to me. An equitable interaction is what has made our friendship.

LITTLE NEIGHBOR EXCHANGES

Another neat exchange I've seen has been between my seven-year-old daughter Christina and her friend Michelle from down the street. The two little girls have become very good friends. Michelle is an only child—quite a contrast from our family. When they visit each other's houses, each girl gets something unique. At our house, Michelle loves the interaction of lots of kids and the chaos that always seems to be a part of our home. Christina, on the other hand, loves to go to Michelle's house to play alone with just her friend and not all her brothers and sisters.

And while their friendship may have its ups and downs, in the long run Michelle and Christina each benefit from the exchange, so they continue the relationship.

THE RIGHT GOSSIP FOR THE RIGHT CUT

Here's a unique exchange which I learned about from my grandmother, who lived in a small rural town most of her life. A local barber had been cutting hair for many years. Even though his fees were reasonable, the barber had one gentleman customer who he never charged. Well, after many years of wondering why this man didn't pay for his haircuts, my grandmother finally asked the barber why. Because he knew her well, after swearing her to secrecy the barber told my grandmother the secret. There was an unspoken exchange between the barber and this customer, who knew *all* the gossip in the county.

As the barber *slowly* cut his hair, the gentleman shared all the latest gossip. For the next month, the barber in turn would share this gossip with his other customers. And he had very loyal customers—because they also wanted to know what was going on locally. Everybody benefited, except those who were being gossiped about!

CROCODILES AND PLOVER BIRDS

We can also find beneficial exchanges in nature. The Egyptian plover, better known as the "Crocodile Bird," has an interesting exchange with the crocodile. The crocodile actually lets this bird get into its mouth and pick out bits of food and leeches from its teeth, kind of like a feathered toothbrush. The crocodile benefits by having clean teeth; the bird benefits by getting food.

Here are some typical human, everyday exchanges: *If you cook the dinner, I'll wash the dishes. If you sew my dress, I'll baby-sit. If you scratch my back, I'll scratch yours.*

Take a moment to think about and write down the exchanges you have with your teenager.

_____

_____

_____

_____

_____

_____

_____

_____

_____

_____

_____

_____

_____

_____

_____

_____

_____

_____

_____

_____

_____

_____

ALL EXCHANGES ARE RUN BY RULES.

Parent's Rule:
If I give you a room,
the the least you can do
is keep it clean.

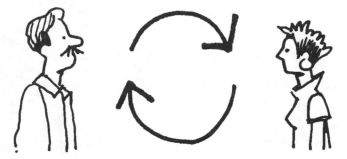

Teenager's Rule:
It's my room, and I can
do anything I want
with it.

STEP TWO:

EXCHANGES ARE RUN BY RULES

In any exchange between two people, each person has his or her own rules that govern the terms of the exchange. This is true for every relationship we have. And while it is easy to see these rules in impersonal exchanges, such as financial transactions, buying a car or getting a loan, it is harder to see the rules that govern the emotional exchanges we have with family and friends. But no matter the relationship, the rules of the exchange are always there, directing the interaction. These rules may be sensible or crazy, but either way, they run all of our relationships—especially those we have with our teenagers.

Here are some rules I've seen in people around me:

- *If you keep buying me things, I will be your friend.*
- *I deserve to be in relationships only with people who treat me as inferior.*
- *If I am the center of attention, then I will come to your parties.*
- *Once you belong to our institution, we have the right to control your life.*

- *The Boss: "If you enjoy your work, you will work harder."*
- *The Employee: "If I enjoy my work, hell must be frozen over."*

Here are some rules I've noticed between some well-intentioned parents and their teenagers:

- *I'll give you anything you want; in return you will love and respect me.*
- *It's a parent's job to do everything for a child.*
- *You should find some way to get rid of the other kids, because I should be an only child.*
- *I should raise my kids exactly like my parents raised me, and I'll get the same results they did.*
- *Every person is a Child of God, except him.*
- *I owe my kids the experience of becoming self-sufficient adults who can think and act for themselves.*
- *Everything my parents have will eventually be mine.*
- *I can use my deceased parents as scapegoats for my failures.*
- *Since I'm your mom, I'll always know what's best for you.*
- *Because you are my parents, you have an obligation to buy me a new car.*

MY "WHAT YOU OWE YOUR KIDS" RULE

One of the basic rules that directs the exchanges I have with my own children is this: *I believe that a parent owes a child the basic necessities of food, shelter, clothing, nurturing and love. Beyond the basics, everything else should be worked out through an exchange.* My kids need clothes, and they should be given those clothes regardless of what they do or don't do for me. But designer clothes are a different story, and an equitable exchange needs to be worked out. My kids must eat, but again, eating *out* is another thing—an exchange must be arranged.

Because of their own personal rules, I've seen some parents give and give and give until they are empty, only to turn around and give some more. Their children don't seem to think about what they can give in return. I know of one mother who repeatedly hands money to her son, only to have him swear at her because it is not enough. Respect should be part of the exchange. Appreciation too. This mother gets neither. Her rule may be the opposite of mine. It is probably something like this: *My son should have all he needs and wants, and I should feel like a failure because I can't provide him with more.*

Along these same lines, I remember one father's comments to his son who had repeatedly insulted him in front of others at a family reunion. It was one of the best responses to an inconsiderate teenager I've ever heard. The father, looking puzzled at his son's behavior, asked, "If you treated your friends like you treat me, how long would your friends be your friends?" *The teenager's rule about earning friendship didn't apply to the relationship he had with his father.*

CRAZY RULES

The unspoken rules that run some parent–teen exchanges are often so one-sided as to be absurd. If you wrote down those rules and showed them to some parents, they wouldn't believe anyone in their right mind would have such one-sided interactions. In fact, they'd probably think that people who followed such warped rules were totally nuts or just plain stupid. But those parents are the *owners* of those rules!

For example, look at the one-sided rules which totally dominate these parent–child exchanges.

Between one father and son, the rule of the teen is: *Whatever trouble I get into my dad will get me out of it.* Complementing the teen's rule is the father's rule: *I will fix any of my son's mistakes; he is just a kid and needs the best start possible in his life.* These two rules driving the relationship between father and son have lead to some interesting, heated exchanges with the police. I don't think the police have the same rules as either father or son. The police rule is probably something like this: *Lock this cocky, spoiled kid up and lose the key; put a gag on the father's mouth and hide his wallet, then things will be much safer and quieter for the rest of us.*

A rule that many adolescents have is "I get to set the rules in my relationship with my parent." Many times I have seen angry children because, for some reason, they have learned that they have the right to be in charge and expect you to conform to their agenda. I'm not saying that their needs should not be met or that they don't get things that they want, just that an equitable exchange should be set by both parties, though the parent is still in charge.

A friend of mine has a teenage daughter who has had a pretty good life. Their family life is easygoing, financially they are fine, and so on. Things were going well until the father became unemployed. Suddenly things weren't so rosy. The daughter had never had to deal with not getting the things she needed. Her parents were now under considerable stress, and tempers were short. After several weeks of this, the daughter was not coping very well. She had learned the rule that "Everything should always be good; if it's not then I can do whatever I want to compensate regardless of how it affects those around me." One day a friend at school told her she had some pot and wanted her to smoke it with her. She complied thinking this might be a way to deal with her problem and that she would be justified in doing it because of the problems at home. This would now cause considerably more stress at home since the girls were caught smoking the pot.

One of the rules I have about friendship with my children is that friendship means respect. I don't use or impose my will on my friends. My children are some of my best friends, but I don't use them as substitute adult friends. This would be disrespectful of our relationship and of who they are. I'm not their friend the way their school friends are. I'm not sixteen, and I am their mother. Friendship without respect isn't real friendship. Yet if respect is present, it is one of the most rewarding exchanges you can have between you and your child.

TRY A TEST?!

What rules govern your exchanges with your teenager? More specifically, what rules govern what you are willing to do for your teenager? What rules does your teenager use to govern what he or she is willing to do for you? What rules govern what you expect from your teenager? What rules does he or she use to govern what is expected from you?

Take some time to answer the following questions. What do you think are your rules are for dealing with your teenager? What do you think your teenager's rules are about interacting with you? Using this list will help you as we continue through the steps.

What Are Your Rules for Dealing with Your Teenager?

1. _____

2. _____

3. _____

What Do You Think Your Teenager's Rules Are for Dealing with You?

1. _____

2. _____

3. _____

WHERE DO WE GET THESE RULES?

All exchanges teach rules. As we interact or exchange in life, we learn the rules that govern our thinking. We interact with family, school, the media, and on and on. As parents, whether we like it or not, our exchanges with our children are teaching them rules. As our children get older, they will learn more and more from other places. Nevertheless, we are always picking up rules through our exchanges.

For example, let's look at the "standing-in-line" rule. Years ago, I attended an educational conference where the majority of attendees were women. Before one of the classes began, I was standing in line when a man in front of me smiled and began chatting. We talked for a minute or two, and then he asked me, "What class is this?" Smiling, trying to hold back a laugh, I said to him, "This is the women's restroom." First shock, then total embarrassment came across his face. Turning away he mumbled, "Oh, I just follow my wife wherever she goes." He then quickly wandered off to find another line. *Standing in line is a rule we all learn culturally; just blindly following his wife is what this man learned from interacting with her.*

I have seen many parents of young children do everything for their child that they believe will benefit the child. They constantly take the child to ball games, athletic practices, music lessons, parties and movies. This is great, but they are also teaching their child a rule such as "Mom or Dad should let me do all the things I want, and these things are most important." Now that this child has learned this rule, what happens when a thirteen-year-old daughter wants to go with a seventeen-year-old boy in his new car. Even though the parent sees that this is probably not going to be very beneficial for the daughter, the daughter's rule is that her parent should let her do what she wants. Now how does a parent of a teen help her change her rule?

We learn many of the rules that drive our exchanges subliminally. Watching television teaches many of us that *all of life's problems can be comfortably resolved in thirty or sixty minutes.* Playing computer games teaches many more of us that *we can be a god in our own little world.* Being with friends as a teen may teach some that *friends are the only ones who truly value me.* And on and on we go, gathering rules as we move through life, then expressing them in all our relationships.

READING THE RULES DIRECTING THESE EXCHANGES

You may begin to understand some people's rules if you watch for the consistent pattern they follow. For example, I heard my daughter's little friend say to her: "If you liked me, you wouldn't go to Melissa's house; you would only come to mine." She often says variations of this to all her playmates. This little girl's rule is *demanding exclusivity in her friends*. Or take the example of kids after they get home from trick-or-treating. When they start to eat all their candy, the obvious rule that they are following is: *If a little bit of something is good, then a lot of it is even better.* Later in life this very same rule resurfaces: *If I like Chinese food, then the all-you-can-eat buffet will be even better.* How many of us now wish we could follow Mary Poppins' rule of "Enough is as good as a feast"?

Rules run our lives by directing the exchanges—and relationships—we have with others. Some of these rules especially dominate exchanges with our teenagers. I don't see most rules as particularly bad or good, but I do see them as either working or not working. Once you understand the rules governing the exchanges with your teenagers, you should keep using them if you are getting good results. If you're not getting the results you want, start changing the rules. Step Three will show you how.

SOME RULES GOVERNING
EXCHANGES ARE HIDDEN.

Some rules are out in the open and on
the table: *"If I give you a room, then the
least you can do is keep it clean."*

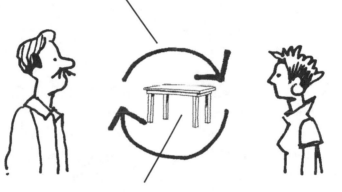

And some rules are hidden and under the
table: *"You owe me because you're the parent,
and that's what parents are for."*

STEP THREE:

SOME RULES GOVERNING EXCHANGES ARE HIDDEN

Some of the most important rules governing our exchanges (relationships) are hidden. We aren't even aware of them. They often are unstated assumptions about what we expect of ourselves and others. When teenagers, for example, operate according to hidden rules, they usually have little awareness of the rule, which may be buried deep in their subconscious. Or they may be vaguely aware of a hidden rule, without recognizing it for what it is. Hidden rules typically have more power over relationships than do "out-in-the-open" rules. They operate independent of any conscious effort and can control parent–teenager relationships, invisibly directing both adult and child to repeat the same problems and conflicts. These problems and conflicts continue as long as the rules remain hidden.

When I was fifteen, for example, I kept finding myself in an unresolvable situation with my mother. If it was Saturday, my work was never done. My mother would give me jobs such as vacuuming or folding clothes. I would do my chores with the expectation that I could do my own thing, such as watching television, when I was finished. But when I *was* finished, and sitting on the sofa watching TV, my mother would come into the room and give me another job to do. I dutifully did whatever she asked me to do.

The thing that frustrated me was that no matter how many jobs I did, my mother always found another project for me to do. When I finally had had enough, I asked her to write down a list of every task she wanted me to do on Saturdays. She agreed that when I finished the jobs on the list, I would be free to do as I pleased. The next Saturday I rushed around finishing all the work she had given me—in less time than she expected. Guess what? When I finished and went outside to play, she found another job for me to do.

Today I understand the hidden rule that governed our exchange. My mother's hidden rule—hidden even from herself—was that *everyone should always be busy and not waste time.* My belief conflicted with her rule; I figured that after I got my work done, I should be free to stare at the ceiling if I wanted to. Having had this experience with my mother, I make it a point to give my children time and permission to express how they feel in their exchanges with me. I also let them bring *my* hidden rules out in the open.

BEATING UP DAD!

Rob, who was nineteen, had been out on his own for a year. During his absence, his father, Steve, had divorced and remarried. Steve and his new wife, Tara, invited Rob to live with them while he attended school at a nearby community college. Rob accepted the invitation. Steve and Tara provided him with tuition money, room and board. They also gave him a pickup truck to drive, along with gasoline, insurance and repair money. In addition, Steve hired Rob to work for him on weekends in his construction business. This was a great deal for Rob. But there was a "hidden" catch. Steve was very active in their local church. He and Tara expected Rob to behave as a model child and demonstrate to the community their success as a Christian family. This was their hidden rule. Rob had no idea that this rule was part of the exchange. Perhaps he was supposed to "get it" through the subtle messages he was being sent. Steve and Tara, on the other hand, probably had no conscious awareness of their rule.

Consequently, Steve and Tara were upset that Rob stayed out late at night with his friends and refused to attend church with them. Rob became the target of their constant recitation of everything he was and wasn't doing. One day Tara confronted him, insisting that he attend church, participate in family activities and arrive home by 10:30 on weeknights. Rob, used to being on his own, resisted. Steve overheard the argument and joined in, taking Tara's side. The more his parents insisted, the angrier Rob became. Finally Rob became so furious that he beat up his father. The dad ended up in the hospital with bruises and broken ribs. It took weeks for him to recuperate. The parents demanded that their wayward son leave the house.

Such violence was out of character for Rob. Why was he so angry? I believe it was because the rules of the exchange were so deeply hidden that he had no way even to discuss them. Therefore, things kept boiling up inside of Rob. With no way to acknowledge or vent what was happening to him, Rob exploded. If Steve and Tara had told him up front what they expected of him in exchange for their generosity, he could have decided for himself, in advance, whether he wanted to accept the conditions attached to their gifts. As it was, their generosity was a trap.

The previous story may seem harsh, but if there are hidden agendas or rules, many teens feel trapped. They seem to be in trouble, and they aren't even sure what they have done. This is what makes this step of the process so valuable to a working relationship with your child. It gives you a tool to see where some of the conflict and "rebellion" may start.

THE FAMILY COUNSELOR'S FAMILY

Cynthia, a counselor and therapist who occasionally gives presentations at seminars on parenting, is herself the mother of two teenage daughters. Her hidden rule is *parents should give, give, give to their children.* Her new husband, Ray, struggling in his equally new role as a stepfather, operates with a similar hidden rule: *I want my stepdaughters to like me, so I will give them whatever they want, whenever they want it.* The girls lived like princesses: trips to Mexico, trips to Disney World, nice clothes, lots of spending money.

Late one evening the girls arrived at their house with two rough-looking boyfriends and asked for some money and the keys to the car. Their intention was to buy booze and get drunk with their friends. Ray handed over the keys to his new car, gave them a handful of money out of his wallet and sent them on their way with the admonition, "Be home before daylight." (He wasn't joking.) The girls had an accident with the car that night; fortunately, no one was seriously injured, but the car was totaled.

Cynthia still presents herself professionally as an expert on parenting, even though her own children's lives are completely out of control. Ray's hidden strategy—to get the girls to like him—failed. One stepdaughter moved out to live on her own; the other moved in with her natural father. In this exchange, the parents foolishly assumed responsibility for the consequences of their daughters' conduct, and the daughters greedily took advantage of their parents' excessively generous hidden rules. In the end, neither the parents nor the daughters got what they really needed.

"IN A MINUTE!"

One way that governing rules stay hidden is that many times people hide their intent. Statements of intent confuse the reading of rules. Let me explain. How many times will a parent ask their teen to do a quick job such as taking out the trash only to have him reply "I will in a minute." I'm sure most parents can relate to this experience. The child's statement of intent is that he will do it sometime in the future and we as parents tend to believe that he wants to do the job only when it's more convenient for him. My own experience is that the hidden rule of the teens is that they really never intend to do the job, and if they put it off, maybe they can get out of doing it or only with further coaxing. As a parent, we read the rule of our child as being willing, yet the hidden rule may be just the opposite.

I recently visited with a friend and talked about this process. She told me about a friend of hers who is having quite a hard time with his son, who had just completed his freshman year at college. Apparently this young man's grades were not very good, and he had done a lot of drinking and partying. She said that his father had given his son everything he needed such as a new car, an apartment, money and so on. In questioning my friend about why his father gave all of this to his son, she said the father didn't know what else to do. He had felt very guilty about not spending enough time with his son and wanted to make it up to him. Again, a statement of intent hiding the real agenda. If the father was sincere in wanting to make up to his son about not spending enough time, why doesn't he spend more time with him? If the father is not willing or able to spend more time with his son, why doesn't he simply tell his son that and let him know that he can't spend time and that the only thing he has to offer is money?

Don't be blinded by statements of intent. You will be able to better read people's rules if you watch their actions more closely, than by relying on what they say they are doing.

A CALLING HIGHER THAN A MERE MOM

Last week I went to lunch with one of my sisters. We began talking, and the subject soon turned to children. She told me about her eighteen-year-old, Jacob. Jacob is a good kid, so good in fact, that he consistently volunteers his time with numerous church activities, helps anyone in need and attends the local community college. He also prides himself on playing in a rock band. The problem, according to my sister, is that Jacob never does any work around the house. She asks him to help, but he ignores her. She finally got to the point of saying, "If you will just put your dirty clothes in the hamper, I'll wash them for you." "No can do!" was his reply. When she finally pinned him down and asked why, he said, "Now that I'm eighteen, I don't need to help anymore. Besides, I play in a rock band, and I'm too busy with more important things."

There are Jacob's hidden rules. Since he is now an "adult," he doesn't need to help anymore (at least not at home). He is now so important that his time is more valuable than his mother's, who works full time and has four other children. Jacob is involved in great work. He helps so many people that he doesn't have time to help in his own home. Now that my sister knows what his hidden rules are, she can start to deal with

Jacob in a real way, and not in his world of illusion. She can begin to set up equitable exchanges regardless of his age or commitments.

RULES RULE RELATIONSHIPS

These stories show how people follow their own rules, hidden or not. These rules are what govern most behavior, and they are rarely about equitable exchanges with others. The next section of the book shows you how to devise new rules and exchanges that will benefit the relationship between you and your children.

PUT ALL THE RULES ON THE TABLE.

Put all the rules on the table . . . and talk about them.

Hidden rules can sabotage your goal of having an effective relationship with your teenagers.

STEP FOUR:

BRINGING ALL THE RULES (HIDDEN OR OTHERWISE) GOVERNING ANY EXCHANGE OUT ON THE TABLE, ALWAYS ALTERS THE EXCHANGE

As long as rules remain hidden, they will control the relationship, usually in ways that produce conflict. If you want an immediate change for the better in your relationship with your teenager, the best way to do it is to bring the hidden rules, all of them, out in the open. With the rules out in the open, both of you can see them, examine them, laugh at them (if appropriate) and change them (if necessary). The benefits that follow will be greater than you can imagine.

Some of the rules teenagers use in their relationships with their parents are pretty absurd. On close examination, some of your rules as a parent might also be pretty silly. Remember, sometimes the most silly and possibly damaging rules are the ones we aren't aware of. The following example from the family of a close friend will illustrate what I'm talking about:

When David was about thirteen, he adopted the practice of objecting whenever things didn't go his way. Consistently, his objection contained the words, "That's not fair!" When asked to take out the garbage, he responded, "That's not fair; I have to do more work than my brothers and sisters." It was the same when treats were divided among the children: "That's not fair; they got more ice cream than I did." He had a hidden rule. If he got more stuff or did less work than someone else, that was just fine, but if he got less stuff or did more work than someone else, it wasn't fair. He was blind to the fact that in the long run, things like goodies and chores tended to even out quite well, and often in his favor. His father sat down with him and helped him to identify his rule so he could examine it. They brought the hidden rule out in the open. Once he (and his siblings) saw how silly the rule was, he dropped it. He never again said, "That's not fair."

By putting the rules on the table, where everyone can see them, you can then honestly deal with what is really going on in your home. Many parents of teenagers feel frustrated when trying to work out situations. Many aren't even sure why it *is* so difficult. (It wasn't so hard when the children were little was it?) Likewise, most teens are totally unaware of where the parent is coming from and most don't *want* to know. But by using this Step Four, everyone is empowered. Both the parents and teen can bring up any hidden rules or issues.

ON THE RECEIVING END OF A SALES PITCH

Step Four can quickly help change problems for the better. I've seen too many times when kids don't get their way and blame the parent. You may think you are doing them a favor or helping them, only to have them get even more upset than if you had done nothing. Let me give you an example of how you can make this type of interaction more positive.

I love going to garage sales, and I've converted my children to them as well because they can see that their money goes a lot farther there than at a store. A few weeks ago, my ten-year-old "teen" kept asking me if she and her friend could go with me. I finally said yes and off we went. We stopped at a few sales, then at one that was quite unique. I believe that the "twenty-something" salesperson was straight from MTV. The first words out of her mouth were directed at these young girls: "How would you like to look sexy?" She then proceeded to show them endless halter tops, shorts ("short" is an under-statement), tops (Band-Aids cover more), and anything else that a stripper might like. Well, these girls were drooling. The seller then turned to me and said, "You're the kind of mom who wants your girls to look cute, aren't you?" All I could hear next was, "Can I, can I?"

I then began to inform everyone that I wasn't that type of mom, and I didn't want my daughter wearing this type of clothing. Immediately, I was the one in trouble. My daughter was embarrassed and upset, and I had to be punished for my inconsideration. She now had her arms folded and was mumbling angry words under her breath.

In the past, this scenario would have ended by our going home, with my child feeling angry and with me feeling guilty. But the scenario didn't end like that. I brought up our exchange right there at the sale. As soon as my daughter began telling me what I was doing wrong, I asked her: "Who was the one who asked to come? Whose car are we driving? Who's paying for the gas? Who has bought you the things that you already got this morning?"

I brought up everything that I was doing and asked why I was the one in trouble. Immediately, my daughter's attitude shifted. "Never mind," she said. "I don't need these clothes. I'm okay." We all went home much happier than if I hadn't brought up the rules.

The success of the previous encounter was built on a single idea: Bring the hidden rules out into the light of day. Bring them out where they can't be ignored or avoided, where responsibility has to be faced. In our home, doing this has changed negative behavior to positive action. Even when an exchange seems small, it can still teach children to stay real and open, which can be very helpful later in life. The following story happened to a close friend of mine who saw how bringing up hidden agendas changed a close relationship.

Marriage Bait

Maggie was dating a young man who was very serious about wanting to get married. She was very clear about letting him know that she just wanted to date without any long-term commitment. One day they were shopping. Maggie noticed an expensive piece of exercise equipment that she had wanted for quite a while. She mentioned this to her friend, and he purchased it for her. But weeks went by, and she never saw the equipment. In the meantime, I asked her to act as a "guinea pig" for me while I practiced my new seminar. When I began teaching the step regarding "hidden rules," a light went on in her head. She realized that her friend had a hidden agenda. He would give her the exercise equipment contingent upon her marrying him. He never told her this when he bought it, only that it was for her. Soon after this she confronted him with this hidden agenda. He didn't know what to tell her. He skirted the issue and even denied it. Within days he broke off the relationship (and never gave her the exercise equipment).

THE MOST DANGEROUS HIDDEN RULE: I CAN DENY THE REAL RULE I'M IMPOSING

It can be very dangerous to the parent–teen relationship if a parent denies the *real* rule he or she imposes. An exchange-based approach only works from the top down: from management to employee; from parents to teens. It doesn't work from the bottom up. Parents initiate and set the rules for most exchanges. Parents are naturally in the power position. If a child sees that a parent is being unfair in the exchange or that he or she is not being truthful and the parent hides his or her real intent, the teen will be frustrated and feel powerless to change things. If a child is not being honest, the parent can deal with it and fix it because of the parent's position.

I recently visited with a struggling teen and his mother. The teenager was trying to express what the problem was between the two of them. He haltingly explained how his mother contradicts him in most situations. The mother immediately replied that this wasn't true. She denied with her own words the very thing she was doing. What is this teen to do? He is not in a position to change or even talk about the real rule. He is stuck. This is why a hidden rule, especially coming from a parent, can be so detrimental to furthering any worthwhile change.

A PARENTING PROCESS THAT PRODUCES RESULTS

You can achieve incredible results when you help children understand the hidden rules in exchanges. Several weeks ago, I had to work some overtime. As a result, the kids needed to help more with cooking and watching the younger children. When payday came, I said, "Let's go shopping for some of the clothes you need, now that it's getting hotter." I bought each of the kids one or two items that they needed. As soon as I agreed to get them something, I was bombarded with thanks. I must have heard over thirty thank-yous. Then I brought up the exchange that allowed me to take them shopping. "The reason I can buy you these clothes," I said, "is because I worked overtime. The reason I could work overtime is because you all helped at home with the work I would normally do. By you helping me, I can help you."

With everyone aware of how this exchange worked, the children knew that there was a cost to what they were getting. They didn't just demand I buy them clothes because I'm the mom.

They were grateful that I worked extra so they could have clothes that they liked. By using this process, you, too, can help your teens become more aware and grateful.

A Simple Exchange for a Thank You

A coworker of mine invited one of my daughters to go with their family for an outing. They had a daughter the same age as mine. Afterwards, my friend and her husband kept talking about how courteous and appreciative my daughter was. They had never met a child who showed so much gratitude. She had even been concerned that they might be spending too much money on her.

Of course this made me feel good. I am proud of my children. I could say it's just genetics, or it's because they are wonderful people. But I know that by having my children aware of hidden costs and exchanges, they are more grateful for what they get and want to give more to others in return.

When teaching my seminars, I often have parents ask me how I can expect these things of my children when all their friends follow different rules. Some people have even asked if my children are embarrassed around their friends because our family is so different. My answer, I believe, surprises them. Many of my children's friends spend more time at our home than at their own. We do have a lot of fun, and we all get along pretty well. When this exchange-based process works, it begins to feel very natural. My children don't do without; they simply share the responsibility of seeing that they get the extras they want.

Seeing and Acknowledging the Exchanges Going on Around Them

Awareness does change things. My children are more aware of the exchanges they have with me. They have learned this because we consistently bring the rules of exchanges out in the open, for all to deal with. Because of this, my kids just can't ignore the obvious: They must do something for what they get. They must take part in the exchange, if only to say, "Thank you."

FOCUS ON GETTING EXCHANGES TO WORK.

Parent   Teenager

FOCUS *your attention on getting the exchange to work.*

DON'T FOCUS *your attention on fixing your teenager.*

Work only on improving the exchanges you have with your teenager, and not on changing your teenager as a person.

STEP FIVE:

FOCUS ON GETTING EXCHANGES TO WORK

Many parents attempt to solve problems with their children by trying to change the child. For example, a mother whose teenagers keep their rooms messy might try to make them be more tidy. She might do this by preaching to them, reminding them what they should do and how they should act. Then the mom becomes frustrated and disappointed when her approach doesn't work. Meanwhile, the teenagers feel threatened and become resentful. But by focusing on the *exchange* which underlies the room-cleaning rule—instead of focusing on the child—parents can have cleaner rooms and happier kids.

Step Five has helped me immensely when dealing with my teenagers over a variety of issues. My burden as a mom is lighter, because I don't have to preach or nag; it's not my job to change my children. They are responsible for what they do or what they become, not me. And they are happier, because each of them is free to be his or her own best self, unhampered by concerns about my approval or disapproval. Our interactions consist mostly of developing exchanges that are mutually beneficial. It is incredible what happens. Here's an example.

THE PIERCED-EAR RULE

The rule I go by when my daughters want pierced ears is, "You can get your ears pierced when you are old enough and responsible enough to take care of them." They show me this by being responsible enough to bathe, keep their hair clean, etc., without my reminding them. I let them know that trips to the doctor for infections will be on their tab—or else they will have to let their holes close.

Linda, age fourteen, got her ears pierced without consulting me first: not a serious problem, provided she was aware of the rule. Next, she wanted more piercing, along the sides and tops of her ears in the cartilage area. I reminded her of the rule and informed her that with pierced earrings in the cartilage area, there was even a greater risk of infection than with earrings in the lobe. It is true that I did not want my daughter to have ten pierced rings in each ear, but I ignored my wants and focused on the exchange.

If I had focused on her instead of on the exchange, our discussion would have turned into an argument over her appearance. My disapproval would have implied an unwillingness on my part to love and accept her as she is. By focusing on the exchange, I avoided all that. I refused to allow her to burden me with the consequences of an unwise decision. She knew she had full responsibility for her choice. And she chose to forego the additional piercing.

Always judge your exchanges, not your child. Even more, value the exchange first, not necessarily the child personally. There are other times to show personal appreciation, but when dealing with an exchange, focus only on that. This may seem a bit impersonal, but this step of the process is very beneficial in building a strong relationship between you and your teen. Let me give you some more examples.

COOL CUSSERS

One Saturday morning, I was cleaning the house and helping Andy, my four-year-old, tidy up his toys. He filled his arms with more toys than he could possibly carry. When he missed the toy box where we kept them, the toys crashed to the floor. He then let out a couple of choice words that I had never heard him say before. Shocked at first, I then realized that he really had no idea what the words meant. I asked him not to use those kinds of words anymore, and he innocently replied, "Okay, Mom," and went back to picking up his toys.

After a little investigative work on my part, I realized where he had picked up his newfound vocabulary. I found the culprit in his older brother, Paul, and his friends. It seems that some of Paul's teenage friends had used some off-color language when they visited our home to play computer games. Andy happened to be around and overheard them. Wanting to act like the big boys he followed suit.

I spoke with Paul, offered him an exchange and clarified the rules of the exchange: "You can use the computer, if your friends don't use that kind of language over here. You guys are teaching Andy how to swear, and he thinks it's a really cool thing to do. By having your friends over, I have to clean up Andy's vocabulary. Either the swearing stops, or you guys can't use my computer."

I didn't have to fight with Paul or get on his case about being a bad example or having terrible friends. I focused on the exchange. Guess what? It worked. Paul took the responsibility for correcting the problem and let his friends know the new rules. I didn't have to. Andy's language soon reverted back to that of a typical four-year-old. The situation was easily resolved, without me having to nag.

NAME-BRAND STUFF—THE OBJECT OF HER DESIRE

Getting a full-time job made it possible for me to buy a few nice things for my children for the first time in quite a while. Juliana, sixteen, was especially pleased with the Dr. Martens shoes I had bought her. For me, though, my combined responsibilities as single mother and breadwinner were rather overwhelming. It seemed the children were doing less and less to help around the house, and the burden on me was too great. I gathered the children together and explained how I felt. I told them I needed more help with the housework. I needed them to do it without me having to remind them. I could see that the children weren't very pleased.

Juliana was in tears, and said, "We shouldn't have to do more housework just because you decided to go to work." (That had been her hidden rule.) I then asked where she thought the money came from to buy the kind of shoes that she was wearing. I then added, "I guess I could quit my job and do housework full time, but if I do, no more Dr. Martens."

Juliana saw that there was a cost to having the shoes that she liked, and now she can play a part in paying that cost by being part of the exchange. She agreed to help around the house and was happy to do so. By again focusing on the exchange, my problem solved positively, without negative words aimed at my kids. This process really works well because it increases your teens' awareness of costs: They share in those costs and learn to be more responsible for what they get.

TWO DIFFERENT OBSESSIONS—WRESTLING AND LONG SHOWERS

My daughter Emily is a World Wrestling Federation fan. I am not. Nevertheless, that is her choice. I allow her to have her choices, if they are not harmful to herself, and if others don't have to pay a cost because of them. But I do require an exchange when she wants to watch wrestling on a TV that I have bought, or view cable channels that I pay for, or use my Internet access. The exchange I require is that she not become isolated in the world of wrestling. She must interact with the family and with me to use these things. And our exchange works great!

Many parents reading this may already be functioning this way. I have parents tell me at my seminars that this is really nothing new except they are now more aware of what they are doing, and they can now help their children become more aware as well. Awareness is a key, especially for your teens. This is what helps build responsibility. This next story will show how teens can take responsibility for what they want, instead of being upset that they don't get everything their way.

Another daughter, Juliana, loved to take long showers in the morning before school when she was sixteen. The problem wasn't that she wanted to take long showers; the problem was that there were eight of us in the house and only one bathroom. In the mornings, everyone needed to use the bathroom. And everyone was complaining to me, wanting a solution.

My first inclination was to get on her case for being so selfish and inconsiderate. But by staying with the exchange rule, I put the responsibility on her to come up with a solution. She did. Since the shower curtain was not see-though, she agreed to leave the bathroom door unlocked so the family could use the bathroom. This worked and everyone got what they needed. I know, since I have five daughters, that this wasn't an easy choice for a sixteen-year-old girl to make, but it gave her what she wanted.

THE $100,000 DEPOSIT

The last story which illustrates the concept of focusing on the exchange, not on the person, is one that my friend Steve told me about himself and his son. Steve found that by bringing up hidden rules and focusing on exchanges, he got what he wanted in his relationship with his teen.

My sixteen-year-old son had begun to hang out with a group of boys who didn't seem the type of friends he usually had. After spending some time with them, he started getting into more trouble than not. This was very uncharacteristic of him and hadn't happened before. Things escalated to the point where he stole a pair of Levi's. When a security guard saw him put the Levi's over the pants he had on, he took off running, and out ran the guard. When my son jumped a fence, he ripped the jeans.

My problem as a parent was twofold. One problem was I didn't want my son to be with these types of friends, because I could see where they were headed. The other problem was that I had to pay a cost for his choice of friends. I had to deal with the police at the front door. I was up late at night wondering when he would come home and in what condition. Since my suggesting that I didn't like his friends and he should find new ones only made him more determined to keep them as friends, I realized that I should use a different approach.

We lived in a rural community where my son worked for a local farmer. Since our family had lived there for many years, the bank gave my son an ATM card. One day he decided to impress his friends by using his card in front of them. They were impressed, since none of them had cards, which were relatively new at that time. Well, my son thought, why not impress them even more by making a deposit. He decided to deposit $10.00, but as his friends egged him on, that amount quickly became $100,000! His friends thought he was great.

The next day the bank called us to find out what happened. In the end, they charged my son's account a $20.00 service fee, and he only had $23.34 in it in the first place. This was a great time for me to bring up the hidden rules of his friends. Now he began to see that they would only be his friends if he would do things that got him in trouble.

I asked him if losing his money was worth having these types of friends. He replied that it wasn't worth it. He finally started to see that the cost was too great and that he should find new friends. I never said any more, but I did notice that after this experience, my son's friends started to change, and so did he.

AN EFFECTIVE TOOL TO HELP YOU WITH YOUR TEEN

I hope the preceding stories have demonstrated what I mean by focusing on getting exchanges to work, instead of continually trying to change your teenager. Even though these are simple stories, I have seen parents in similar situations focus directly on their kids and never resolve a thing.

In my house, I have easily resolved the same situations *and* improved my relationship with my teens. I have seen my children taking responsibility instead of getting angry. My load is lightened, and my friendship with my children continually grows.

THE BENEFITS OF EXCHANGING WITH YOUR TEEN

So far, I have given you a five-step process to use when interacting with your teens. First, realize that all relationships are exchanges and second that theses exchanges are run by rules. Some of the rules that govern exchanges are hidden. You then need to put all the rules on the table. And finally, focus on getting exchanges to work.

Now, the real surprise is that there are hidden benefits in using these steps. This is part of the "secret." Not only do you have effective tools to work through difficult problems, our teens actually can change for the better in the process. Let's look at just some of these hidden benefits.

INCREASED MUTUAL RESPECT

An incredible change that I have seen in my children is the increased respect they have not only for me, but for each other. Since they are now more aware of how each person pays a price for what he or she needs and gets, my children try harder to help each other. They have more consideration for one another as well. They always show gratitude for the things I do for them, because they now know that I don't *have* to do it for them. Awareness makes such a difference!

If you think about it, aren't people generally nicer to you if you have something that they want? If someone has something you need, you certainly don't deliberately offend them, do you? This is what is happening in our home. We all want it to work, and everyone is aware of the impact they have.

Sometimes, raising children is like trying to make it across a big lake with the entire family in a small boat. Everyone needs to work together to get to the other side. I know some teenagers who might jump up and down in high heels in this small boat because they were angry about having to help. They don't realize that they could sink themselves and everybody else. Both kids and parents need to realize that the family is stuck in this small boat together. By rowing in unison, everyone can make it to the other side.

INCREASED SELF-ESTEEM

What teenager wouldn't benefit from increased self-esteem? As your children become involved in working exchanges, they feel a sense of accomplishment. My children are more confident about their choices and themselves. Responsibility becomes an everyday reality, instead of a nebulous concept that adults talk about.

Recently, there's been a lot of debate in the media about parents taking responsibility for their children and their children's actions. Instead, perhaps parents need to take a more active role in helping their children take responsibility for what they do. As kids become aware of the price they pay for their actions, and the exchanges they must make to pay the price, perhaps they may be less inclined to be irresponsible.

. . . AND A LIGHTER LOAD ON YOU

I don't know one parent who doesn't want their load lightened. Raising kids, especially teenagers, is difficult work. When

I was in school and carrying a tremendous load, I realized that my children were the only ones around to help me lighten it. After all, the load was much heavier because of them. So I shifted much of my day-to-day tasks over to them. I had no choice. But through that experience I learned about a valuable tool—exchanges—which can help any parent. Knowing that their teens are actively helping resolve problems offers over-loaded parents considerable relief.

AND MORE

I'm still discovering more hidden benefits in using this dynamic management approach with my family. Working with it is an ongoing process. Since my teenagers still manage to come up with new situations needing different exchanges, I'm constantly learn-ing innovative ways to more effectively use the system.

SHIFTING TO AN EXCHANGE-BASED APPROACH

An exchange-based approach for dealing with teenagers can eliminate the emotional power struggles between you and your kids. You can negotiate exchanges with your teenagers that work for everyone involved. Raising a teenager can then become a whole lot easier.

Using this approach, you don't try to "control" your teenagers. All you need to do is control your part of the exchange, for everyone's benefit. This new kind of relationship between you and your teens is what I call an *exchange-based relationship*. As I mentioned earlier, all relationships are based on exchanges, whether you are aware of it or not. In an exchange-based relationship, you and your teenagers deliberately focus attention on getting your individual exchanges to work.

Memorize or write down the five steps that define the exchange-based approach. Or put them on a card and post it in a prominent place, so you can see them on a daily basis.

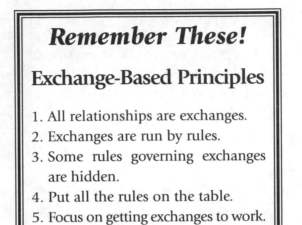

Remember These!

Exchange-Based Principles

1. All relationships are exchanges.
2. Exchanges are run by rules.
3. Some rules governing exchanges are hidden.
4. Put all the rules on the table.
5. Focus on getting exchanges to work.

When you were comforting that little infant in your arms, did you ever think that he or she would one day grow up and talk back to you?

MAKING THE CHANGE WITH YOUR TEENAGER

The other day, when I was flipping through TV channels, I saw at least five infomercials for weight loss. Each one claimed to have the magical answer for anyone wanting to lose weight. One infomercial even promised, "This is the miracle you've always been waiting for!" I thought to myself, if these programs are so good and have even worked for some people, why don't more people lose weight (myself included)?

The answer, I concluded, is that there are costs associated with losing weight that many people aren't willing to pay: You can only eat certain foods; you have to exercise; you must take herbs, and so on. Personally, I have found that a protein-based diet works very well for me. I am able to lose weight quickly, and I feel great. So why don't I stay on it all the time? I don't want to pay the price of never having nachos and or pizza again.

Weight loss is a good metaphor for how successfully you apply the concepts in this book. Effectively using an exchange-based approach may be easier for some parents than for others. Your success depends on how you apply these concepts and how willing you are to stick with them.

Also, there are costs associated with using these concepts. For the remainder of the book, I talk about these costs and demonstrate how to effectively use an exchange-based approach.

IMPORTANT POINTS TO CONSIDER WHEN USING EXCHANGES

Here are a few important guides to help you make the transition to an exchange-based approach with your teenager.

• It Costs to Change

If a ball has momentum and is going strongly in a particular direction, a certain amount of energy must be applied to that ball to move it in a different direction. It is a law of physics, and it is a law of teenagers. I remember once when we had to move. My older kids dragged their feet, whined, complained loudly and tried to convince me not to move. But regardless of the kicking and screaming, we moved anyway. After we lived at our new place for a time, I heard these same whiners say, "I like where we live now much better than our old place." There is always a price to pay for making any transition. Everyone, regardless of age, tends to resist change, even if the change is beneficial.

Changing your relationship with your child, to one based on exchanges, will extract a cost. Even the promise of a happier, more productive family life won't make much difference to your teen's attitude. You would think because teens are young and flexible that they would like to try something new to make things better. Maybe some do, but maintaining the status quo is often a stronger force than you can imagine.

ONE MOM WHO PAID THE COST OF CHANGE

I know of a mother whose children just ignored her and any efforts she made to help them. She would cook, clean and do laundry while the rest of the family watched television or played with friends. Over time, she finally woke up to how bad things had become. She decided that is was time to have more equitable exchanges. The problem was, she couldn't budge anyone into helping her. In fact, they just ignored her. Finally she stopped doing *everything*.

The laundry piled up to the ceiling, the dishes were headed in the same direction, and the family started having hunger pangs. The kids and her husband cried and pleaded. The mother held her ground and did nothing. It wasn't easy, but her strike was effective. The rest of the family tried every trick they could to get her back into the old routine, but she wouldn't budge.

Finally, after two weeks of soiled clothes, dirty dishes, a chaotic household and empty stomachs especially, the family capitulated. An exchange was worked out where everyone in the house did his or her share. No one member had to carry the entire load. Everyone was so glad to have things work out that each family member actually did his or her job.

In the future, just the threat of another strike moved this mother's family back into action. This was the price this mother had to pay to have a more equitable exchange with her family. But she paid the cost, and having done so, she got her equitable exchange.

• Keep the Exchanges Honest

Karin is a wife and mother who feels she always has an important mission to accomplish. She likes being a leader and helping others, no matter the context. She also believes that her family's job is to support her in this. When she leaves to speak or meet with people, her family is supposed to assume her responsibilities at home. What confuses her family is that there is never any specific cause Karin is dedicated to; she just seems to be gone a lot. Up until a few years ago, when Karin would go, most of the load fell on her oldest teenage daughter, Brittney.

Brittney was very reliable, always tending to the kids, cooking for the family and doing other things she felt her mom should do. With her mother frequently gone, Brittney was over-whelmed by all this responsibility. Karin in turn would try to explain to her daughter: "I need your help because what I am doing is so important, and this is how you can support me."

But Brittney never agreed to this exchange; her mother imposed it on her. She had no free time, and even her school work was affected. I watched this situation go on for years, time that Brittney should have been learning, having fun and doing things with her friends. Instead, she had to be a mom.

I guess Brittney finally had enough. One day she just left. She eloped with her first real boyfriend, a boy her mother didn't even know existed. Brittney wrote her mother a note, packed her bags and left.

I was around when Karin was crying to a group of women as

she told them about Brittney. "After all I've done for her," she said "this is all the thanks I get. Now I'm going to have to watch the children by myself." Tears streamed down her face.

Karin had worked out an exchange with her daughter that was a con job. Brittney had no choice in it and received almost nothing in return. Karin liked telling people that she had a large family, but she really didn't like the responsibility that went with it. Karin used guilt and parental pressure to get her daughter to do her job. There was never any honest discussion between the two of them to work out an equitable exchange. Finally, when Brittney had had enough—she left.

If you want exchanges to benefit all those involved, being honest is your only choice. If you expect this approach to work, neither you nor your children can lie. In many relationships, the rules that direct exchanges are deceptively hidden.

As the parent, you must be willing to give up whatever hidden agendas you might have in your relationship with your teenager. Put all the rules on the table. Your goal is to create an atmosphere of equity, where everyone clearly understands the rules. Without honesty, success is impossible. Parents need to take responsibility for the rules they impose and not deny that they are doing it.

STOPPING THE LIES

When my son Paul was sixteen, he had a girlfriend in a nearby town. Of course, he wanted to spend time with her. He asked to use my car to drive to her house so they could do their homework together. I consented, provided that he buy gasoline for the car and return home by 10:30 at night. He kept the agreement at first, but soon he became careless about the curfew, often arriving home several hours late.

Paul regards himself as a very honest person, yet he wasn't being honest with me by not keeping up his end of the agreement. So one day I told Paul that I had a problem with him. He asked what that was and I replied, "I want to know why you are lying to me." His reply was, "I don't lie to you. When did I do that?" I replied, "You lied about our exchange. You told me you would bring the car home by 10:30. That was our agreement. Since you haven't done that lately, you've broken our agreement, and it looks to me like you are lying."

Immediately Paul understood what I meant. After that, he either arrived home on time or called home to renegotiate his arrival time. By helping Paul see that he wasn't keeping up his end of the agreement, I was able to quickly solve the problem without getting into an argument.

Honesty gives power and security to a relationship like nothing else can. It is the anchor that holds everything together. Honesty helps provide a safe and stable environment where everyone can focus on what they really need, instead of playing games.

- **Remember! You're in the Power Position**

Remember that you, the parents, are in the power position. You make the money. You own the home. You have the knowledge. I've seen too many parents who believe they've lost control. Many feel as if they are driving down a one-way street, going the wrong way, with a crazy juvenile at the wheel.

An exchange-based approach, however, helps parents regain their natural control. Instead of dictating to their children, parents can instead use their personal resources (time and property) for mutual benefit. This natural power, used wisely, eliminates power struggles and focuses attention on getting exchanges to work.

In the business world, an effective manager would never let employees with little or no experience dictate how the company is run. And the reason employees are generally willing to do as they are asked is because they are compensated for their efforts. All parties have agreed to a mutually beneficial exchange. This same approach can be used with your families. The parent usually has something that the teenager wants, such as time, assistance, money, a car. This puts parents in the power position, able to make exchanges with their children, not visa versa.

OUR FEARLESS, DIAPERED LEADER

Last fall, some relatives stayed with us for a few days. Before they left, they needed to do some shopping before their trip home. Four adults and a two-year-old set out for the store. As we entered the store, the two-year-old led the way. First, he wouldn't ride in the cart; he wanted to walk. Then he noticed a drink stand off to his right, and he wanted a drink. His mother attempted a deal with him: "You can have the drink, if you ride in the cart." The deal fell through. Now we had a tot walking even slower, alternating between a suck on his straw and a step ahead. And, here were the adults—all bent over and staring at the drink cup as it teetered on the edge of disaster—slowly walking through the store behind our two-year-old leader.

Eventually my relatives found the aisle they were looking for. The toddler put the unfinished drink down in the middle of the walkway and decided to rearrange the products neatly stacked nearby. As his mom grabbed the stuff and put it back on the rack, the kid streaked to another display. Then it was his dad's turn to pick things up. Then all four of us were helping. If we took anything away from him, he screamed. All of our attention was centered on him. In the middle of this chaos, it dawned on me what was going on. We were letting a two-year-old dictate the schedule and behavior of four adults!

After all was said and done, it took us over an hour to buy something that should have taken five minutes. This is a silly, but typical, story. Parents allow behavior like this all the time. We let kids set our agenda for us. We relinquish our power. How could a parent have done things differently using this exchange process? How do you teach your child new rules of the exchange?

If this had been my child, I would have asked him if he wanted to go in the store with everyone else. If so, I would have explained that he would need to ride in the cart the whole time. As soon as the whining started, I would have immediately taken him to the car and waited until everyone else came out. There really wasn't a reason to have four adults in the store anyway. This action would begin to teach this child the rule that he isn't the one setting the exchange for situations. There is a price for a parent to pay initially, that can prevent and change many future problems. It would have been easier to pay the cost of having sat in the car with this toddler than to have him learn the rule that he was in charge of the entire shopping adventure.

When setting exchanges, something to remember is that you have many valuable resources to give your child. Your time, money, attention and friendship are just a few. When I exchange with my children, one priceless commodity that I want from them is respect. I also very much enjoy the friendship they are willing to give me. In return, I also try to have respect for them and treat them as my friends.

Exchanges can be made regardless of your financial status. I used to buy their favorite foods with food stamps and make them meals they liked in exchange for baby-sitting help. I've exchanged my playing board games with them for help folding clothes. Parents with a lot of money shouldn't owe more to their children than anyone else. Parents should use whatever means they have available to help their teen make some rewarding exchanges. Use what you have to help them learn responsibility.

• **Establish Simple Exchanges with Your Children** *Before* **They Reach Their Teens**
I recently took the children to the dentist for their regular checkups. A few days later, the dentist's receptionist called me

at work with an unscheduled opening for Christina, age six, to have some cavities filled. In the small town where we live, the dentist's office is only open two days a week. It's located across the street from the elementary school where Christina goes to kindergarten. My workplace is a forty-mile commute from there, so it would have been very difficult for me to take Christina to the dentist. The opening was for later that same day so I accepted, hoping I could work it out.

I called the elementary school to have them tell Christina about the appointment and ask her to go to the dentist's office across the street at the appropriate time. She followed the instructions without any fuss or difficulty. The staff at the dentist's office was amazed at how mature and responsible she was, visiting the dentist's office alone at such a young age, getting her teeth drilled and filled, and then returning to school. I realize that this is not a typical situation for most parents to allow a young child to go to the dentist by herself. I certainly wouldn't do this where I now live. This was a very small, safe town and the staff knew our family very well. I knew the school would alert me if there was a problem or if Christina was hesitant to go to the dentist by herself.

Christina is very independent for her age. I attribute much of her maturity to the responsibility she has learned by my using an exchange-based approach in the family. She is now taking responsibility for her own health and well-being. She was very proud of what she had accomplished that day and couldn't wait to tell me when she got home. She realized that she helped me out and made my life easier.

One thing I have realized, with all that I've been through, is that parenting many times is doing what works best in a situation and not always acting from a preconceived pattern. Parents need to be flexible. Helping your child learn responsibility through exchange will help them to be a more livable teen.

• Put the Burden for Solutions on the Teenager

When your teens need something, let them be responsible for figuring out how to get it. Most kids will try to make the parent figure out all the exchanges. Once your teens realize that it is their responsibility, it actually is kind of fun to see them set the rules of the exchange. My oldest daughter, Juliana, was on the high school golf team. I always knew the night before she had golf practice, because she would be cleaning the kitchen and doing all the dishes. She knew if she did that, I would let her use the car the next day to take her golf clubs to school. The really neat thing was I never had to even ask her to do it!

When your teen comes asking for something, you may want to ask questions like: *"If I do this for you, what do I get in return?"*

Or, *"Why should I?"* These questions may seem a little harsh, but the alternative may be having your teenager take advantage of you. Once the exchange-based pattern is firmly established in your family, however, you will see your children approach you with an exchange, instead of a request or a demand.

BMWs AT THE DMV

While I was working at the Department of Motor Vehicles, a consumer economics teacher at the local high school gave his classes an assignment: How would they spend a million dollars in thirty days? Of course, many of his students decided to "buy" expensive cars such as a BMW or a Mercedes-Benz. And it naturally followed that they needed information on the costs of registering and licensing such cars.

Our office fielded more than fifty phone calls in two weeks from people requesting such information. Of all the calls, only one was from an actual student. The rest of the calls were from parents who were doing their children's schoolwork for them.

I feel that parents should shift some of the load that they carry on behalf of their children back to the children them-selves. For many reasons, such as guilt or wanting the best for our children, we may instead be denying those we love the most the things that would make them stronger—including taking responsibility for their wants and needs.

• **Have Flexible Rules**

Keep the rules in your exchanges with your teenagers flexible. If you have teenagers, you know how dynamic and fast-moving their world is. Nothing stays the same. Your life will be much easier if you can adapt the rules to your teenager's changing world. I have a general rule that says *we can change the rules.* Of course, rules shouldn't be arbitrarily changed on a parent's whim. When changes need to be made, let all of those affected know why change is necessary and how it will benefit everyone.

DAD'S GOING TO BUY ME A CAR

A rigid rule can have you and your family stuck in a dead end. I have a friend who helped his oldest child purchase a used vehicle. It became a rule among the older kids: *Dad is obligated to help buy and maintain each child's first car.*

As the months passed, this father could see it wasn't working for him. He bought the vehicle, and he was paying for gas and repairs. The insurance was ready to bankrupt him. He began to see that this exchange was not benefiting him much. So, calling this car-buying venture a learning experience, he decided not to do it for his other children.

Several months later I visited again with this friend. What he told me that happened later was very interesting. "At first my son loudly complained while the car sat in the driveway for a couple of weeks. Since he didn't have money to buy gas, he finally went out on his own and got a job. He was now able to pay for his own gas and insurance. The car no longer 'needed' all those repairs he wanted done. Next, I sat down with everybody who had a vested interest in having a future car. I told the other kids that our financial circumstances had changed and we couldn't afford to buy everyone a car. To be honest, I even told them how stupid their dad was buying this car in the first place. They were reluctantly okay with it all, and I surely was relieved."

This father revised the rules. Because of the changed circumstances, he could no longer be held hostage by a rule or kids holding him to that rule. To me, I don't care if you buy your kids five cars or no cars, just that the rules and exchanges work for everyone. By keeping rules flexible, you can adjust your exchanges to fit the situation. With teenagers, your life is always in a state of flux just like the rules should be.

• Be Consistent in Your Exchanges with Your Teenager

I believe that consistency is the most important factor in raising kids effectively. Consistency gives your child a barometer to measure where you are at (or what they can get away with). As the parent, you must assume the responsibility to be consistent and to reset the terms of exchanges whenever necessary.

I know of a mother who tried an exchange approach but couldn't stick with it. "I tried this with my kids years ago," she told me. "I even went on strike once to get them to stop taking advantage of me. It worked, but only for a week. When I quit putting the pressure on, everyone else quit as well."

Being consistent is like tending a garden. A garden must be constantly cultivated or the weeds will quickly take over and ruin all the hard work you have done. It's the same with exchanges. Sometimes I forget and slip into old ways of doing things. I have to catch myself and correct my course. I know that my children will cheerfully take whatever they can get from me, whenever they can get it, without an exchange. So I must regularly be consistent in our exchanges.

• Hold Your Ground

"Stop right there, young man!" Stevie looks at his mom out of the corner of his eye and continues doing what he wants. Stevie's mom tries again. "Don't you move another step! No, No, N-N-O-O!" she continues. Moving a little slower now, but still watching his mom, Stevie keeps right on moving. "I mean it, don't even think about it," she tries again. Without looking back, Stevie continues on his way. His mom, now weary of the whole situation and countless others like it, shrugs her shoulders. Then, in a tired voice, she says, "He never listens to me." And you know what? He doesn't have to. Nothing will happen to little Stevie. He hears the words, the threats, but nothing else ever happens. No spanking, no time out, no restrictions. Just the same old words without actions.

Never set a rule that you are not willing and able to follow through with. If these interactions between little Stevie and his mother continue until he is sixteen, and little Stevie becomes Steve, what has his mom trained him to do when interacting with her? If you said ignore her, you're probably right.

I have a friend who grew tired of her husband threatening their kids when they acted up in the car. When the kids were tousling with each other in the back seat, Dad would say, "If you don't stop that, we'll let you walk!" Or if the noise level got too high, "One more scream from you and we'll make you get out of the car." Did the kids ever listen? Of course not. They may have been in the middle of the Mojave Desert when the threats were made, but the kids knew that their dad would never really make them walk.

Finally, my friend had enough of her husband's inconsistencies.

One day, after picking the kids up at a ball game two miles from their home, the fighting began as usual. Again, the dad made his threats. But this time, my friend followed through and made her husband stop the car. The two teenage boys actually did have to walk home (they lived in a safe neighborhood). They (and their dad) were fuming. The mom's doing this shocked the *whole* family, but from then on, the parents never had to make threats about walking home.

• Make Sure the Exchange Is Clearly Understood

Always be clear about what your exchanges involve. Sometimes I find that some of the clarity and meaning in an exchange can be lost between the world of a mom and that of a teenager. Let me illustrate with the following examples.

I had a sock problem with my teenage girls. They were wearing my socks, and I wasn't. I would go to my sock drawer, and it would be empty. I had to go my girls' room, find their socks and sort out which ones were mine. I did this over and over again. Until one day I thought of a solution.

When I had some time I gathered all my socks together. Using a permanent laundry marker, I wrote the word "MOM" on all of my socks. I believed that I had solved my sock problem. Everyone would now know whose socks were whose. But a few days later, as we sorted the family wash, my sock solution came under question. My fourteen-year-old daughter was helping me sort the clothes and found my labeled socks. With a puzzled look on her face she said, "Mom, why is the word 'WOW' on some of these socks?"

You may never know how your teenager perceives what is so clear to you. Before putting exchanges into action, therefore, it is best to clarify the rules of the exchange with everyone involved.

To use another example, my son Paul, who was seventeen at the time, had been letting his household responsibilities slip. I had to remind him of the terms of our exchange. Paul wasn't very happy about this and began complaining to a visiting friend of mine. "I have so much going on at school," he moaned, "with homework and football practice. There's no way I can help around the house as much as Mom wants me to. I just don't have enough time."

My friend saw that Paul genuinely felt overwhelmed, so he asked him, "Can you spare one-half hour a day? That's all she's asking for." Paul's facial expression immediately changed. He then agreed, stating, "Oh, I can do that."

"I think Paul assumed you wanted him to participate in some sort of slave labor camp," my friend later told me. In fact,

Paul just needed to have the terms of the exchange quantified in units that he could relate to. He needed to know what the limit was on the contribution expected of him. Paul needed his mother to make sure she was clearly being understood.

• Avoid Being Held Hostage

Don't be held hostage by a perceived obligation to uphold some value as a parent. Many parents have an abundance of guilt about not doing enough or being a good enough parent. This makes them susceptible to manipulation by the media, by advertisers and especially by their kids. I've seen little kids manipulate parental guilt into quite a return for themselves. By the time they are teens, they have this manipulation down to a science.

I remember a fourteen-year-old girl commenting on all the "stuff" her parents had given her. She was giving me a tour of their beautiful Victorian home. The tour ended in her own room. It was full of everything: a new bedroom set in one corner; a television and video recorder in another; big stuffed animals everywhere; and a large closet full of clothes and shoes. She even had her own beautifully decorated bathroom. As she sat on the bed, the most tired look came over this girl's young face and she said, "I just don't know what I'm going to push my parents into buying me next."

In another story, a women I know came to me seeking advice. She bought her eighteen-year-old working daughter a new car, at the daughter's urging, while she herself still drives a clunker. Now the daughter wants the mother to pay for the insurance, too. The daughter has pressured the mother with the notion that "a mother is supposed to help her children!" Sure you want to be a good parent, but beware of letting a smart teenager decide for you what constitutes good parenting. Sure you want to be a good parent, but what is your real motive as a parent of a teen?

• Decide What You Want the Most

I have seen many parents run themselves ragged, taking their children to every activity and organized sport that exists. From one day to the next they are at piano lessons, dance lessons, soccer practice and Boy Scouts. I see nothing wrong in having your children participate in these activities. But what I do see as wrong is the fact that many parents do all this out of guilt, believing that they need to expose their children to many activities in order to be a good parent. They believe that somehow their children will be culturally deprived if they don't participate in as many things as possible.

I had to fight the same guilt when I didn't have the time or resources to provide these experiences for my own children. While my son Paul was growing up, I never enrolled him in an organized sport league. Nevertheless, he ended up playing football at Princeton University, an Ivy League school. He really doesn't seem to be suffering too much from cultural deprivation.

Do what is most beneficial to everyone, but make sure you understand what rules are driving your behavior. In my case, I decided my children needed a sane mother more than they needed Girl Scouts. That was my motivating rule.

As I talk to parents about these ideas, I have realized that what one parent wants from his or her teen is as unique as teens themselves. Some parents just want to make it through the day without a phone call from their child's school. Others want their children to win beauty pageants. Some parents want good grades for their children. Others just want to be good friends with their kids. Everyone is different, and everyone's "wants" are different. And what makes the exchanged-based process unique is that it gives parents a tool that can be used in all of these situations.

Once you understand this, then you need to take the time to really decide what you want. Clearly defining the most basic desires within your family can give you a foundation on which to set your exchanges. If having a clean house is paramount to you, then set your exchanges with your child to help you get that. Find out what your children want, and use that in your exchange to get your house clean.

• **One Last Point: Exchanges Extend Outside the Family**
As your teens learn to use this process, they will apply it to other relationships in their life without even knowing it. This can be very helpful to them, especially as they go out into the world and learn to survive. It may help them avoid being taken advantage of, because they will be aware that reciprocity should be a part of all their relationships.

To use an example close to home, one day I overheard my teenaged daughter visiting with her best friend. Her friend had asked her one too many times to give her answers for her homework. My daughter pointed out that the friend never did that for *her*, so she wouldn't do it for her friend. The girl was upset and didn't talk to my daughter for a few days. Finally she called up and apologized. She realized that she had been taking advantage of the friendship and said she wouldn't do it anymore. They are still best friends to this day.

I hope the points covered here will help you implement and successfully apply the exchange-based approach with your teens. The most important rule to follow is: Do what works best for you and your family. Of course, deciding what's best for everyone can be difficult, and the issues of responsibility and "blame" often rear their heads.

EXCHANGES YANK TEENAGERS OUT OF THEIR FANTASY WORLDS

As I was watching the news yesterday, a commentator was talking to an "expert" about a recent high school shooting. He stated that there had been far more public response to this shooting than to any other news topic he had ever covered. One of his main points was that this shooting had taken place in an area that many people would say is the "American Dream," a safe place. The question was then asked, "How could this happen to these kinds of people in this type of neighborhood?"

Blame seems to be the topic of the day. People blame the movie industry, the media, the Internet, schools and lax gun-control laws for much of the outrageous behavior that many teens display. But after all the dust clears, parents seem to be the *ultimate* target for such blame. In spite of all this finger-pointing at parents, I see very little specific, practical help offered for solving parent–teenager problems.

I am not a psychologist or a sociologist; I am a mother. And I believe that parents owe it to their children to teach them to take responsibility for their actions. I don't believe that we can blame society, the media or insufficient laws for the behavior of our children.

My children are Hispanic, have been on welfare, have watched their parents divorce and have been raised by a single mother. Statistically, my children are at high risk for becoming high school dropouts, using drugs and generally being out of control. They are none of these things. The reason that I even bring up the issues is that perhaps the media and "experts" are wrong about the causes of outrageous behavior. In the midst of the plethora of blame, I would like to offer a solution: Use my exchange-based approach to teach kids to be responsible for themselves. Here are some pointed illustrations of just what I mean.

LOST IN WORLDS OF THEIR OWN MAKING

Have you ever noticed that the parents of the Peanuts characters don't ever say anything. It's just "wa, wa, wa, wa." That's all they ever say. And I think this is all that many teenagers hear. Just the dull, droning sounds of endless words creating meaninglessness. Most uninvited noise seems to be an intrusion into their worlds.

Many teens are trying to define themselves. They are leaving the world where they looked to their parents as a role models. Now they look to friends, television, movies and other types of media for defini-

Teenagers naturally create fantasy worlds.

tion. The problem with that is much of it is not real.

One of my daughters believes that everything she sees on television or the Internet is true. I have tried to explain to her that this isn't so. One day she began chatting online with a "boy" who seemed too good to be true. He supposedly lived nearby. He had recently moved here from the same place we used to live. He was just the right age, and so on. She asked me to come look, because she wanted to know if she could give him her phone number. I was a little suspicious. I told her that she really had no idea who she was talking to. "Yes I do," she said. "He told me right here," pointing to the screen. She wouldn't believe that this person wasn't who he said he was.

Two days later, her teenaged female cousin confessed that she had been pretending to be this boy.

My daughter had been in a fantasy world. To her it was real. Many teens tend to do the same. They are looking to the constructed images of the media to define themselves and their world. But these images are just that, images. For example, many young girls are obsessed with losing weight. I've known girls who look gorgeous and still think that they are fat. Magazines and movies provide the models of beauty that they aspire to. Many kids spend most of their waking hours in front of some kind of screen. This electronic fantasy world becomes the model of how life is to be lived. If teens are allowed to stay in these worlds, without having to come out and deal with reality, then their fantasy world becomes warped to the point that they believe it's reality.

WRECKING THE DRIVER-TRAINING CAR

I have a friend whose teenaged daughter totally wrecked her driver-training car. Her instructor was looking for a pen he had dropped on the car floor. The young girl turned her head totally around, while still driving, and began talking with her friend riding in the back seat. She didn't turn her head back again, but kept talking. Nobody saw the horse walking across the road until it was too late. Luckily no one was hurt, except the horse. This is an example of what some teens do. They become so involved in their own little world that they ignore the real world outside the driver-training car.

Earlier I referred to a high school shooting. According to media reports, the two boys who did the shootings had been totally immersed in violent movies, music, computer games and Internet sites. They then transferred the blood and gore of these mediums to the floors of their own high school. How did this happen?

Before the tragedy occurred these teens had to acquire or have access to numerous things: guns; materials to make bombs; computers with Internet hookups; televisions; propane; trench coats; and ammunition. How did they pay for these things or even make some of the transactions? My guess is that they were just given the resources—by parents and others—to make these transactions without an exchange.

But if the boys had been required to make exchanges for these transactions, especially with their parents, then the parents might have been more aware of what their sons were doing. These boys would not have been able to stay so secluded. They would have had to share the real cost of what they were doing.

Some parents actually help their teens maintain a fantasy world. And then by some miracle, they expect their children to become responsible adults. Expecting this kind of miracle is also a fantasy. Something realistic must be done to help our children function in society. An exchange-based process can help you do that.

WORKING YOURSELF OUT OF A JOB

Being a parent should be a temporary job. Of course you will always love your children, and you will always be their parent, but letting them go is also part of your job.

I know a couple who want to be parents forever. They have four grown children, all still living with them. The children won't leave home. Their parents provide them with a nice house to live in, all expenses paid. These adult children get their clothes washed, meals cooked and house cleaned. They can afford to have nicer cars than their parents. What a deal!

But it's not as good a deal as it appears. To be a permanent parent, you have to have permanent children. These adult children are trapped in dependency, imposed on them by parents who have an unhealthy need to keep their children dependent. What appears to be generosity is really selfishness on the part of the parents.

BEING A PARENT IS JUST A ROLE

Realizing that being a parent is only a job—or role—was a new concept to me. For many years, my life was centered around my kids and being their mom. When anyone asked what I did, it was always the same answer, "I'm a mom."

I gradually realized, however, that I had to begin to disconnect myself as a person from the role of mother. By doing that, I could focus on helping my children become independent of me. I was better able to let them set their own direction in their lives. Someday, when they are all gone, I will hopefully have worked myself out of the job of parent and will simply be my children's friend.

One reason many parents don't have equitable exchanges with their teen is because the teen puts their parents in a set role. Just like if you were to hire a butler to answer your door and drive you around, you always expect him to perform those services no matter what. Many times, teens do the same thing with their parents. They always expect the parents to perform predetermined services no matter what. Often, this does not make an equitable exchange possible. But if you center on making exchanges work within *each* situation, you'll be pleasantly surprised at the results, and the wonderful relationship you'll develop with your child. It can be *really* neat!

What follows is a story from a father telling about a unique experience he had with his thirteen-year-old daughter. His chance to work himself out of a parenting job came earlier to him than it does for most of us.

Years ago, my daughter Amy approached me saying, "I need to talk with you Dad—just you and me." So we talked. Amy began, "Dad, isn't it true that I pretty much do everything the right way?"

"Well, yes, it's pretty much true," I had to admit. She got good grades, did her household chores, stayed out of trouble, helped us with the younger children, and did a very good job of being responsible for herself.

"So let's quit doing this parent–child thing," she said.

Well, he agreed. He didn't quit being a parent or stop loving her, but he did allow her to carry as heavy a load for herself as she could. And it worked. She has done well in life and now is a parent herself. She recently expressed to her father how much she appreciated his respect for her wishes to take charge of her life at an early age. Some parents may not agree that this is good parenting, yet it accomplished early what many parents want to eventually accomplish with their children.

I now have an eighteen-year-old stepson who is deaf. Because of his uniqueness, I will have to take a more active role in parenting for several more years. Each child is different and you go with what each individual child needs most. What you may want to think about is that eventually your goal is to stop parenting even though you never stop being their parent.

EFFORTS WELL REWARDED

When you apply the concepts discussed in this book, you will notice some results immediately. Over time, and with consistent use of the exchange-based approach, you will see a change in your children's attitudes. They will deal with life differently. The following and final story in this book illustrates a change I saw in my daughter that convinced me that this approach was working in her life.

A couple of years ago, I discovered that my fourteen-year-old daughter Linda and her young friends had been having drinking parties. I found out that most of the drinking occurred at the home of one of the friends, Sara, because her single parent was seldom home. I felt a need to intervene, my daughter being much too young to be drinking alcohol.

I didn't confront Linda about it right away. Later that evening, after I called her home from Sara's house, Linda and three of her friends arrived at our house and immediately disappeared into Linda's room. I overheard their conversation as I walked down the hall. The friends were pressuring Linda to do something she didn't want to do, and they advised her to lie to me about it. At this point I interrupted them and sent the three girls home. I let them know that I had overheard them. I sent Linda to the kitchen to do the dishes, which would give her time to think.

Shortly after this I found Linda crying at the kitchen sink. "I need to go away," she said. "I need to get away from these people. They keep making me do things I don't want to do."

We went together to a restaurant to discuss the matter. There were no other girls for her to have as friends, since we lived in a very small town at the time.

"Can you get by until the end of the school year?" I asked, "We will be moving to California then."

"No," she said. "I need to leave now." At the young age of fourteen, Linda had successfully identified the solution to a very difficult problem. Within a week, we had arranged for her to move earlier than the rest of the family to live with an aunt until we arrived. There she found plenty of new friends. The move gave her a chance to blossom in wonderful ways we couldn't have imagined before. She accomplished things I didn't even know she could do.

A month after my talk with Linda, the parents of the other girls were just beginning to deal with the problem. They were planning a meeting for all of the parents to discuss how to deal with their children. At our house, the problem was solved and my daughter was the one who solved it.

I realize that this solution isn't one that a lot of parents could choose. I know that many parents have problems with their teens that involve serious situations such as drinking, drugs, sex, etc. The intent of this book is to help parents who have a fairly healthy relationship with their teens. Yet, there are some teens who have problems that should only be dealt with through professional help and counseling. This book is not intended to solve deep-rooted problems.

But, regardless of what level of relationship or problems you may be having with your teen, this process can still help you. The key is to maintain the consistency of your exchanges with your child. Linda made a major, responsible choice because I had maintained a consistency for many years with her. She learned certain rules in her life. Perhaps your teen will begin to choose to live his or her life differently if he or she knows you will always be consistent and not facilitate wrong choices.

What if a teenage girl *knows* that if she were to get pregnant, her mother isn't going to raise that child or have them live in her home, (or in other words, have mom take responsibility for the teenager's actions). Perhaps then the daughter will know that her responsibility may be for her to have to go to work and take care of the child on her own, get married, give the baby up for adoption, etc. Knowing this can definitely be preventive medicine. Teens who choose to drink, if it is by their own choice or that of their peers, will always need to be responsible for those choices in their exchanges with you as their parent. Are you helping them by letting them have a car to go out? How about giving them an allowance that gives them money to buy these things?

You cannot control your teen, especially as he or she becomes more of an adult, but you can control the consistency of your exchanges. Teens can and will make wrong choices, but you as a parent need to hold true to your rules and exchanges. This consistency is the key to having this process work. Again, raising a teen is difficult; sometimes it is easier than others, but I do know from personal experience that these principles can and do work.

IT'S UP TO YOU

The process taught in this book can be used in many ways. You can use it to solve just one problem you are having with your child, or you can completely transform your entire relationship with him or her. You can even carry this process into other kinds of problem relationships. I had a friend use these ideas on parenting to restructure his entire company. How you use the exchanged-based process is entirely up to you.

Because of the individuality of each parent–child relationship, the results of applying this process will also be unique. What is happening in my own family is incredible! There is a magical quality that has a life of its own. I can't even describe the love, respect and friendship that is present in our home. The contrast of how things were and how they are now after making these changes has been the biggest change that I have ever experienced in my life. But it is uniquely mine. I pray that you will have as much success with your family as I have had with mine.

About the Author

JENNIE HERNANDEZ HANKS is the mother of seven children, four of them teenagers. With years of on-the-job-training as a mother, she is also professionally trained in human resource management. She has worked in both health care and local government and managed a small business for five years. Jennie most recently  worked as the training coordinator for a nationally recognized resort. She is fluent in Spanish, plays the piano and is a pretty good cook.

The Parent's Little Book of Lists

This is a handy reference with practical, kid-tested ideas to help parents deal with everything from monsters in the closet to unsolicited criticism of parenting abilities.

Code #5122 • Quality Softcover • $10.95

Parents, Teens and Boundaries

How parents set boundaries with their teens is one of the most important aspects of the parent-child relationship. Jane Bluestein looks at twenty aspects of boundary-setting and clearly explains when to set boundaries and how to express and maintain them.

Code #2794 • Quality Softcover • $8.95

Safeguarding Your Teenager from the Dragons of Life

Bettie Youngs shows us how to keep teenagers on track toward worthwhile goals by providing the support they need to become responsible, happy adults.

Code #2646 • Quality Softcover • $11.95

Ignite Positive Change
in Your Life and in Your World

Women Circling The Earth

This profound and practical book explains the history and importance of the circle movement and details the benefits of women's circles for: providing a much-needed sense of community; helping people reconnect with the sacred; manifesting healing; achieving consensus; and creating social change.

Code #7559 • Quality Paperback • $12.95

The Evolving Woman

Chronicling the gripping, real-life stories of women's triumph over abusive relationships, this book is a testament to the resiliency of women. An inspiration and lifeline for any woman living the misery of domestic abuse.

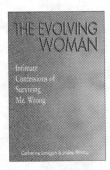

Code #7591 • Quality Paperback • $11.95

Great New Books for the Teens in your Life

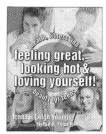

Bestselling *Chicken Soup* for Teens
Collect Them All!